For my Mother, who always encouraged me to
follow my passion. – G.T

For J.P.
With special thanks to the Biology Department
at Boston University. – J.M.

BIG PICTURE PRESS

First published in the UK in 2021 by Big Picture Press,
an imprint of Bonnier Books UK,
The Plaza, 535 King's Road, London, SW10 0SZ
Owned by Bonnier Books
Sveavägen 56, Stockholm, Sweden
www.templarco.co.uk/big-picture-press
www.bonnierbooks.co.uk

1 3 5 7 9 10 8 6 4 2

ISBN 978-1-78741-424-2

This book was typeset in Reina 12 and Otari
The illustrations were created with watercolour

Written by Joanna McInerney
Edited by Isobel Boston
Designed by Kieran Hood
Consultant Dr. Sarah W. Davies
Production by Neil Randles

Printed in China

Made For Each Other

GEORGINA TAYLOR

BPP

Contents

What is Symbiosis?

In the natural world, it benefits to have a friend. Teamwork or an unexpected partner could make all the difference to survival – whether it's warding off predators, removing parasites or aiding reproduction. It is for this reason that creatures great and small come together, from the tiniest of tree frogs to the biggest of elephants. The strength of these relationships gives each organism the confidence to overcome fears, and establish a level of trust and intimacy that would otherwise seem impossible.

In this book, we explore nature's most precious relationships in the form of symbiosis – how two or more organisms have adapted to each other for survival. To understand symbiosis, is to understand the complex and fragile network that all life depends on. If just one link in the chain is removed, the consequences could be far reaching. From the top of the jungle canopy to the depths of the ocean, habitats all around the world are teeming with these extraordinary animal partnerships.

Into the

Monarch Butterflies & Milkweed

There is almost nothing more beautiful than the sight of a butterfly in summer. Vibrant colours and beautiful patterns provide a visual feast as these insects dance from flower to flower. But these bright colours are not merely for pleasure, they have an important job to do – they warn predators to keep away.

With bright orange wings streaked with black markings and white flecks, the monarch butterfly (*Danaus plexippus*) is a species well known for its distinctive colouring. It has a particularly special reason to warn predators away – it is poisonous.

In a unique symbiotic relationship, the adult monarch butterfly exclusively lays her eggs on the underside of the milkweed plant (*Asclepias syriaca*). Just a few days later tiny white caterpillars emerge and begin feeding on the plant on which they were born. These nutritious greens have a hidden benefit – they are highly poisonous. Consuming this plant means that the monarch butterfly will become poisonous to predators, too.

In return, the monarch butterfly pollinates the milkweed – helping the plants to thrive and ultimately providing more nurseries for the next generation of butterflies.

But developing a relationship that is so dependent on one species of plant is both ingenious and perilous. In recent years, the decline in milkweed plants (due to climate change and deforestation) has also attributed to dwindling numbers of the monarch butterfly. As a result, many conservation schemes have been implemented to restore the populations.

Fighting off predators and feeding is essential for monarch butterflies' epic migrations, which see them travel thousands of kilometres every year to hibernate in warmer climates, before making the journey back to their breeding grounds.

Madame Berthe's Mouse Lemur & Phromnia Rosea

Up in the treetops of Madagascar's Kirindy forests, the world's smallest primate is on the move. Darting between branches and tangles of vines, it skilfully leaps distances ten times its body size.

The Kirindy forests are far from luscious. Dry, barren and with fluctuating temperatures, survival here is a struggle, yet this protected reserve hosts many species not found in any other part of the world. It is this forest that the Madame Berthe's mouse lemur (*Microcebus berthae*) calls home. A recently discovered species, this tiny primate weighs about as much as a light bulb, and fits comfortably in the palm of a hand. Despite the difficulties that life in the Kirindy forests can bring, this species is only found here, and its special relationship with its habitat is only now being understood by conservationists.

A nocturnal hunter, Madame Berthe's mouse lemur spends around half of its time sleeping in nests of dry leaves. The other half is spent foraging. Although it often feeds on insects and fruit, this wide-eyed creature also seeks out a secret key ingredient – honeydew – which it needs to survive. It obtains this vital food source from the small, white larvae of *Phromnia rosea*, which also lives here. The insect can only be found on the branches of the liana – a long-stemmed woody vine that grows around trees in the forest. Without the liana, the insect wouldn't be able to produce the honeydew that the mouse lemur craves. Adult *Phromnia rosea* are bright-pink and leaf-like, with tall, flat forewings.

Understanding this three-way symbiosis helps to bring to light the complex and fragile network that all life depends on and the delicate relationships that form between species.

Grey Wolves & Ravens

Their relationship may have been depicted in folklore throughout history, but the symbiosis between wolves and ravens is more than just legend. It is perhaps one of nature's most well-established and advantageous symbiotic partnerships, thought to date back over thousands of years. However, it is only recently that studies have been able to shed some light on this most fascinating of relationships.

The raven (*Corvus corax*) is often revered as one of the most intelligent breeds of bird on Earth. True to this, the ravens at Yellowstone National Park in the United States were quick to learn that by following grey wolves (*Canis lupus*) they could be rewarded with food.

Although food in this vast national park is plentiful, the ravens' inability to bring down large prey on their own means having to rely on their cunning and skill to survive. The ravens know that wolves are far more capable of tackling a large animal, and that even in packs, they rarely consume everything in one sitting. Indeed, it is thought that ravens often consume as much as the wolves.

Undeterred by blood-curdling howls and snarling teeth, studies have observed these clever birds in close proximity to a travelling pack of wolves on almost every occasion. Whether circling in the sky or perched in the trees above, the ravens are always close by.

But it isn't all one-sided. From their aerial views, sharp-eyed ravens have been observed using a series of calls to signal to wolves that an injured animal or danger is nearby. Footage has even emerged of ravens playing with wolf cubs – no doubt seeking to foster a lasting relationship that will serve the two well in later years.

Fallow Deer & Magpies

In woodlands across the world, one of the most picturesque images of symbiosis can be found.

Like a scene from a fairy tale, a herd of graceful fallow deer (*Dama dama*) moves through the thicket and step out into the open meadow. Cautiously, they stop to graze on grasses and nibble at low-lying plants whilst the morning sun dries the dew. Known for their distinctive honey coat flecked with white, and the black stripe on their tail, fallow deer are native to European woodland but can be found all around the world.

The females, known as does, often huddle together as a group, whilst the powerful males, known as stags, form their own herds, called leks. It is only during breeding season, that the two groups interact with one another.

Often whilst feeding or resting in the shade, some feathery visitors greet the deer, too. Common magpies (*Pica pica*), as well as other types of woodland bird, have been observed cleaning the deers' coats of unwanted guests including ticks and other parasites. Precariously balancing on their backs, ends of noses and tails, the birds gently complete their tasks. What's more, the huge antlers of the stags (which can reach a metre across) are the perfect places for the birds to perch.

Ruby-Throated Hummingbirds & Cardinal Flowers

A glimmer of ruby red streaks across the sky, gone in a flash. Reaching speeds of up to 64 kilometres per hour, the ruby-throated hummingbird (*Archilochus colubris*) moves so quickly it appears as little more than a blur of wings to the human eye. Although it is one of the smallest birds on Earth, it takes a huge amount of energy to keep the hummingbird moving at such pace – and this tiny creature needs to consume almost double its body weight in food each day.

The cardinal flower (*Lobelia cardinalis*) is a favourite source of nectar for the ruby-throated hummingbird. The flower's vivacious red colouring is not only attractive to this little bird, but their deep tubular shape is also perfectly suited for long, slightly curved beaks. Like two pieces of a jigsaw puzzle, the ruby-throated hummingbird and the cardinal flower are an exact fit.

In fact, cardinal flowers are so well-adapted to suit the feeding habits of ruby-throated hummingbirds, they don't even offer a 'platform' for animals to rest on whilst they feed. The hummingbirds don't need one – they can hover in the air. Their wings beat at unimaginable speeds of 40 to 80 times per second, producing their distinctive 'hum'. In return for food, the hummingbirds pollinate the cardinal flowers. Because of the symbiotic adaption of these flowers, the ruby-throated hummingbird and the cardinal flower have become almost entirely dependent on each other for survival.

Aldabra Giant Tortoises & Seychelles Magpie-Robins

Located in the tropical Indian Ocean, the picturesque Seychelles are a collection of 115 islands. Aside from tropical beaches and warm climates, they are also famed for the many animals that call the islands home, some of which are found nowhere else in the world.

The Seychelles magpie-robin (*Copsychus sechellarum*) is native to these islands, and is in fact not a magpie or a robin at all. An endangered species, its existence was once threatened by the destruction of its luscious habitat and the introduction of predators such as cats and rats. In fact, its numbers were reduced so severely that it was thought that only 16 birds remained in 1970. Thankfully, much has been done to save this little bird between then and now, and the population has blossomed to steadier numbers in recent years. Although conservation has much to do with its survival, the clever magpie-robin also developed some unique relationships with the other islands inhabitants for its own benefit.

The Aldabra giant tortoise (*Aldabrachelys gigantea*) is perhaps the most iconic resident of the Seychelles. Weighing up to 250 kilograms, this enormous reptile spends much of its time wandering through the shade, grazing on the various plant species that are on offer. Due to its weight, the legs of the tortoise sink into the soft ground, disturbing the soil as it walks. This reveals a feast of tasty worms and insects for the magpie-robin to enjoy, and so, like a faithful follower, it sticks close to the Aldabra tortoise, following it wherever it goes. In return, the magpie-robin keeps the Aldabra tortoise clean, pecking the ticks and parasites out from the folds of its skin.

Beneath the Waves

Hawaiian Bobtail Squid & Vibrio Fischeri

Like a scene from a science-fiction movie, a strange, iridescent light moves by night under the clear coastal waters of Hawaii. But it is not an alien – it is the glow of the Hawaiian bobtail squid (*Euprymna scolopes*), a tiny species of mollusc.

Hunting in open waters at night can be dangerous for a small animal. Seals, crabs and large fish commonly prey upon the squid, but this little creature is a master of disguise. During the day, the Hawaiian bobtail squid camouflages itself against the seabed, covering its body in sand and stone.

But at night, it showcases an exceptional skill. Hawaiian bobtail squid have learned how to create their own light. By harvesting light-emitting bacteria from the seawater, these clever animals can mimic starlight through their skin, casting little more than a faint shadow on to the seabed below. This 'cloak' allows them to hunt virtually unnoticed, thereby avoiding predators and fooling prey.

From birth, Hawaiian bobtail squid learn how to attract and harvest bacteria from seawater. In return for their services, these microscopic organisms, known as *Vibrio fischeri*, live in a specialized light organ in the squid's mantle (the outside covering of the squid's body), feeding on a diet of sugar provided by their host. Every day, the bacteria are expelled back into the sea and replenished with a fresh supply.

False Killer Whales & Bottlenose Dolphins

Sometimes, symbiotic relationships are not about survival. Whilst food, shelter and safety are vital, there are times where friendship is all that is needed to bring members of the animal kingdom together.

A perfect example of this is the recent discovery of the interactions between false killer whales (*Pseudorca crassidens*) and bottlenose dolphins (*Tursiops truncatus*). Until this interaction was documented, little was known about the behaviour of false killer whales (who are not actually whales, but members of the dolphin family). Shy and with declining numbers, it was previously thought these reserved creatures lived in deeper waters, until footage showed a gathering of hundreds of false killer whales in much shallower warm waters off the coast of New Zealand.

But that wasn't all they discovered. Researchers found that the false killer whales had unlikely friends with them too – bottlenose dolphins. Although the two species had joined together in this instance to hunt huge shoals of sardines, further studies showed the false killer whales and bottlenose dolphins were able to recognise one another and greet each other as old friends. In fact, they had well-established relationships that had formed over the course of many years. The two species socialised, travelled and rested together, as well as using their special partnership to hunt and stay safe from predators.

Although it is currently unknown how or when this partnership first formed, it is thought to be one of the first documented symbiotic relationships where the benefit is almost purely social interaction.

Spongicola Shrimp & Venus' Flower Basket

Some of nature's most fascinating wonders can be found at sea. From creatures that make their own light, to vibrant coral formations and symmetrical shells, the seabed is littered with living creatures that twinkle like jewels.

On first inspection, the intricate and complex glass structures of the Venus' Flower Basket (*Euplectella aspergillum*) look like beautiful vases embedded on the sea floor. In fact, these white, lattice-like structures are that of a living sea sponge. Made from crystallised silica, each of these glass 'skeletons' are unique, with no two designs that are the same. The bacteria harnessed by the sponge are also bioluminescent, helping them to glow majestically in the darkness. Although they appear delicate, the Venus' Flower Basket are in fact incredibly resilient, capable of withstanding underwater sandstorms and fast-moving currents. But their beauty hides a secret that is even more enchanting.

Peering inside these glasshouse structures, it is common to find a pair of shrimp (*Spongicola venusta*) living inside. Having entered through the tiny holes in the sponge when they were young, the male and female shrimp quickly become too big to leave. Inside, the shrimp are well-protected from predators and small morsels of food wash into the sponge with the current for them to eat. In return, the shrimp keep the skeletal structure clean. The shrimp's larvae will be small enough to pass through and find a sponge of their own, leaving the two alone inside the Venus' Flower Basket for the rest of their lives.

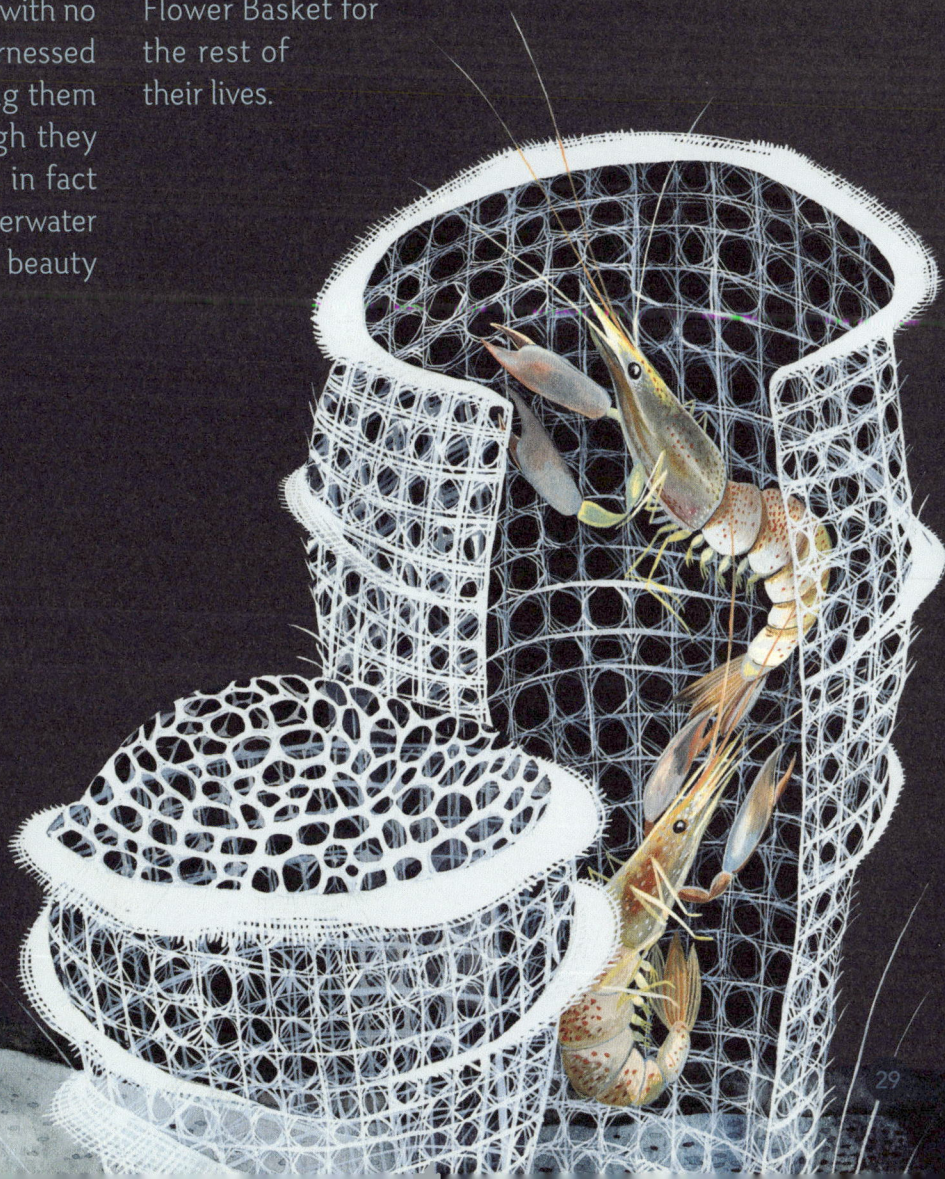

Clownfish & Sea Anemones

Life on the coral reef is never quiet. A riot of colour and movement, hundreds of species coexist with one another here, competing for food and space.

Slowly waving their tentacles in the ocean currents, you'd be forgiven for thinking that sea anemones (*Actiniaria*) are tranquil. However, these beautifully coloured organisms are meat-eating marine animals, capable of stunning and killing small fish with intense, lethal stings. Despite this, one of the most common sights on the coral reef is a busy family of orange clownfish (*Amphiprion percula*) darting in between the tentacles of their sea anemone home. How is it that these fish can thrive here without being attacked? The answer, is mucus.

The clownfish has a thick coating of mucus on its body, which makes the fish immune from the anemone's venomous stings. Although finding the right anemone home can be a challenging process, once this relationship has been established there are a whole host of benefits to be enjoyed.

Like living inside an electric fence, the clownfish is protected against predators, and can safely retreat into its venomous home at the first sign of danger. It also has a safe place to lay its eggs. In return, the clownfish protects its host and the anemone benefits from having a ready supply of food, leftovers from the clownfish's meals.

When young clownfish are ready to leave the safety of their nest, they will need to start a new relationship with a different sea anemone in the same way that their parents did.

Sharks & Remora Fish

ew animals would be brave enough to swim close to a shark, let alone attach themselves to it. But the extremes of the ocean can create strange and surprising relationships.

Remora fish (*Remora remora*) are remarkable creatures, capable of attaching themselves to almost anything that swims by. These underwater hitchhikers use a special type of suction disc at the top of their head to stick themselves on to other creatures, from whales to turtles and even sharks. This suction disc is actually an adapted dorsal fin – the same fin that sticks out at the top of a shark's back – that has evolved over time. Remoras are born with this on their back, but

it migrates forwards towards the head as they grow into adults. It is common to see up to 20 remoras together at a time, catching a ride on a shark as it glides through the ocean. But why would such a small fish want to attach itself to one of the ocean's most fearsome predators?

By not having to swim themselves, these cunning fish are able to conserve energy and also catch an easy meal by feeding on the shark's leftovers. And in exchange for free rides and meals, they provide their hosts with a type of exclusive spa treatment – remoras will happily nibble at any parasites or dead skin, helping to keep the shark healthy.

Pistol Goby & Shrimp Fish

On a sandy bank at the edge of the coral reef, a pistol shrimp (*Alpheus glaber*) is busy burrowing.

Almost completely blind and about 5 centimetres in length, this vulnerable crustacean is a tasty snack for many ocean creatures. But while it may seem defenceless, the pistol shrimp is able to 'fire' superheated bubbles from its claw, that can stun or kill small fish. The sound this produces is thought to be one of the loudest sounds in the ocean. Despite its formidable weapon, the pistol shrimp rarely leaves the confines of its underground home and spends almost its whole life cleaning its burrow – the shifting sands of the seabed mean endless emptying of debris and removal of unwanted intruders. Luckily, the pistol shrimp can rely on an unexpected partner to be its eyes, while it's busy below ground.

About 10 centimetres long, the goby fish (*Cryptocentrus cinctus*) stands guard at the entrance to the burrow, keeping a watchful eye out for predators. This unusual watchman also shares the pistol shrimp's home. Throughout the day, the two remain in close contact – the pistol shrimp constantly feels the goby with its long antennae whilst moving about, and the goby makes sharp flicks of its tail to warn the shrimp of danger. At the sight of a predator, the goby signals for the shrimp to retreat back inside, and the goby quickly follows. In return for its services, the goby is able to live in luxury in a spotlessly clean home.

It is unclear how or why this symbiotic relationship came to be, but it is one of nature's most unique examples of mutualism between two animals.

Marine Iguanas & Sally Lightfoot Crabs

Battered by ferocious winds, stormy seas and scorching temperatures, the creatures that live on the Galápagos Islands in the Pacific Ocean need to be tough, smart and persistent in order to survive.

Famously visited by Charles Darwin during his voyage on the *H.M.S. Beagle*, one of the islands most iconic inhabitants was described by the naturalist as the 'imp of darkness'. Darwin was referring to the marine iguana (*Amblyrhynchus cristatus*) – the only lizard species on Earth that lives and forages by the ocean.

Almost as black as the rocks on which it lives, the marine iguana is perfectly camouflaged with its slippery surroundings.

Warming itself after the chill of night, its tough skin and long claws enable it to latch securely to the rocks to bask and raise its body temperature with the rising sun. This is vital as the iguanas will soon lower their body temperatures again, by diving into the freezing ocean to look for food such as algae and seaweed. This adaptation has meant survival for the marine iguanas, as food on the islands is scarce. However, it is a task that's not taken lightly – cooling their body temperature down to such levels slows the marine iguana's heart rate and they can only spend 10 minutes at most in the water.

In stark contrast to the black and grey tones of the marine lizard, the vibrant Sally Lightfoot crab (*Grapsus grapsus*) displays fiery shades of red and orange dashed with blue. Walking on tiptoes, these agile movers look as though they are dancing across the rocks, moving forwards, backwards, left and right, battling slippery surfaces and ocean spray with ease. But, even the most active of crabs get a little tired sometimes. It is far more relaxing to navigate the tough terrain by hitching a ride on one of the passing iguanas – there might even been a tasty snack, such as a tic or morsel of dead skin, to be had at the same time. This extraordinary and somewhat comical sight is one of the most iconic of the Galápagos Islands.

P

Across the

lains

Ostriches & Zebras

Gathered around a waterhole on the African plains, creatures great and small stop to quench their thirst. The scene is lively, with birds and all manner of mammals standing side by side, like a depiction from Noah's Ark. But life here is never peaceful for long. With water scarce and predators stalking in the long grasses, the creatures that live here need to be vigilant if they are to survive. It can be beneficial to have a friend.

One of the best examples of how two species can work together is the relationship between ostriches (*Struthio camelus*) and zebras (*Equus quagga*). Commonly found together at watering holes and on the grasslands, they are never far from each other's side – and they have good reason for sticking together

Up to 3 metres tall, with a neck making up around a third of its height, the ostrich surveys the landscape.

Its dark, round eyes are the largest of any land animal, measuring 5 centimetres across on average. The combination of excellent vision and great height means that the common ostrich can see moving predators up to 3 kilometres away.

But, what zebras lack in height they make up for in hearing. A zebra's ears are located high on its head, and can swivel in nearly every direction. Their ears are also larger and more rounded than horse's, which means they can collect a greater range of sounds.

Working as a team and utilising their strengths, this dynamic pair can ensure their safety. Grunts, stomps and calls warn one another of any dangers, as well as other animals that are nearby.

White-Winged Doves & Saguaro Cactus

From a perfectly round hole in the side of a towering Saguaro cactus (*Carnegiea gigantea*), a thin beak cautiously emerges. It belongs to a white-winged dove (*Zenaida asiatica*), who has made her nest here. It is a safe place for her and her chicks to shelter from the scorching heat of the Sonoran Desert.

With soaring temperatures of up to 48 degrees Celsius on a summer's day, this area of land in Arizona, United States, is a tough terrain to live in. Lack of food and shelter means the creatures that live here need to be resourceful and opportunistic if they want to survive.

The white-winged dove is one such creature, making extraordinary use of one of the few plants that thrive here – the Saguaro cactus. Standing tall at up to 12 metres, these impressive plants can live to be 200 years old. But not only do they provide shelter from the extremes of the desert, they also do something very special.

Once a year and for one night only, the Saguaro blooms to reveal stunning white flowers. These later develop delicious red fruits, which quench the thirst of many desert dwellers during the hottest season of the year. Perfectly positioned atop the Saguaros, the fruits are in ideal reach of many of the flying birds and bats that pass through the desert. The fruits are a nutritious feast for the dove and are filled with thousands of tiny seeds. Should these be dropped while feeding or as the dove flies the Saguaro increases its own chances for survival by ensuring its seeds are dispersed far and wide.

Olive Baboons & African Elephants

With temperatures regularly exceeding 40 degrees Celsius in the summer, the dry, hot conditions of Eritrea, eastern Africa, mean droughts are common. The animals that can be found here face the challenges of living in this unforgiving place and go to extreme lengths to find water.

The African elephants (*Loxodonta africana*) that live in this region are highly in tune with their environment. Their exceptionally good memories mean they can remember their previously trodden paths and where rivers and watering holes had once been. Their trunk is also essentially a very long nose, which means they are able to smell water up to 20 kilometres away. Luckily these big animals can also survive for up to four days without water and often travel long distances to find it.

Elephants use their detection skills to locate dry river beds and dig down into them, making wells with their trunks and feet. They make the wells big enough for them to bathe in to keep their skin cool, which in turn provides a mini waterhole for other animals.

Olive baboons (*Papio anubis*), named after their greenish grey coats, can often be found sticking close to an elephant herd – they know that this relationship means their family will be hydrated. In exchange for using elephants in their search for water, the baboons will climb trees to scour the horizon, alerting elephants to oncoming danger using a series of screeches and barks. Olive baboons are one of the most far-reaching groups of baboons, found in 25 countries on the African continent, and their special relationship with elephants may well have influenced this.

Oxpecker Birds & Giraffes

The Serengeti is a vast region in eastern Africa that extends from Tanzania all the way to south-western Kenya, covering some 15,000 square kilometres. Popular with tourists, this national park is the destination of a lifetime, complete with crocodile-infested rivers, eagle-filled skies, and elephants, lions and wildebeest roaming the plains. The world's tallest animal also lives here – the giraffe (*Giraffa camelopardalis*).

At over 5 metres tall, with a neck making up nearly half of its height, the giraffe is an iconic sight. Travelling the Serengeti in families of up to 30 members, giraffes eat everything from fruits to buds and seeds. Their mild-mannered nature extends not only to close family members, but to guests, too. They are the perfect hosts – allowing themselves to be plucked, pecked and poked by small birds called oxpeckers (*Buphagus erythrorhynchus*).

These little birds have adapted to a life built around the giraffe and other Serengeti grazers. Their curved, slightly flattened beak is the perfect shape for plucking off parasites, with scissor-like snips. Their feet are also ideally designed with two forward-facing and two backward-facing toes, meaning they can cling on to a moving animal from any angle.

Oxpeckers spend almost all their lives living close to their host – they are even known to pluck some of the giraffe's hair to line their nests with. But these noisy birds can also act as a good lookout for predators. With their sharp eyesight and high perches on the giraffe's neck, they are ideally positioned to scan the plains for danger. The local name for oxpeckers is 'askari wa kifaru', which means 'the rhino's guard' – as they engage in similar behaviour with rhinoceros, too.

Under the
Can

opy

Capuchin Monkeys & Balsa Tree Flowers

White-headed capuchin monkeys (*Cebus imitator*) spend much of their lives high in the Ecuadorian jungle treetops. They are social creatures, with up to 40 members living in one family. Aside from a midday nap when temperatures can soar to around 35 degrees Celsius, these primates can spend almost the entire day feeding. The rainforest provides a rich and varied diet, from nuts, berries and sweet fruits to insects, spiders and birds' eggs. Most importantly for the capuchin monkey, an abundance of flowers can also be found here to devour – studies have indicated that these animals feed on as many as 95 different plant species.

In much the same way that bees pollinate flowers in an English country garden, capuchin monkeys play a special part in the spreading of pollen in the rainforest. Weighing about as much as an apple when fully-grown, white-headed capuchin monkeys are perfectly suited to finding delicate flowers that are hard to reach, or entangled in vines. Pressing their small faces deep into the petals to reach the sweet nectar inside, some of the pollen from the stigma is transferred to their facial fur. As the monkey feeds from flower to flower, the pollen dust is transferred. Some flowers species are particularly attractive to these primate pollinators, such as the flowers that grow on the balsa tree (*Ochroma pyramidale*). With wide, cup-shaped petals and long stamens, these flowers have evolved to ensure as much pollen dust is transferred as possible.

It is not often thought that mammals such as monkeys play a role in plant pollination, but it is true that they have an important role in some South American jungles. In fact, many other species including lizards and birds are also key pollinators for plants – not just insects.

Hardwicke's Woolly Bats & Pitcher Plants

Whilst the most common image of a bat roost conjures up thoughts of dark, damp caves, these are not the only places that bats seek to take some rest. In fact, the tiny Hardwicke's woolly bat (*Kerivoula hardwickii*), prefers a more private place – that of the carnivorous pitcher plant.

Pitcher plants grow in tropical regions around the world. Whilst all pitcher plants are predatory, digesting a range of insects and small animals, the *Nepenthes hemsleyana*is are not as good at attracting meals as its carnivorous relatives. In fact, research has found that the closest relative of this pitcher plant is at least seven times more successful at capturing insects. Biologists believe this is due to the light odour produced by *Nepenthes hemsleyana* which is ineffective in attracting small prey. Instead, these clever plants have adapted to make sure they get their source of nutrients elsewhere.

It is thought that this specific type of pitcher has evolved specifically to attract Hardwicke's woolly bats, and they have good reason for doing so. Although seemingly unpleasant, bat droppings actually account for up to a third of *Nepenthes hemsleyana*'s diet and are a vital source of nutrients, rich in nitrogen and potassium. Without the bats, the plants' survival would be in danger.

Scientific studies show these plants have developed a specific bell shape to their pitcher, which makes them easy to find with echolocation (the way that bats find objects through reflected sound). After a long night of hunting, the woolly bat searches for a snug place to rest by sending out high-pitched calls. These bounce off the pitcher plant, making the plant easy to locate in the dense vegetation of the rainforest. The bats themselves have evolved in response to this symbiosis – their echolocation calls are thought to be the highest of any bat species. They are the only known species of bat to coexist with a plant in this way.

Hyacinth Macaws & Toco Toucans

There are some instances of symbiosis that are not straightforward. The cycle of dependence in nature can sometimes be both necessary and devastating.

The Pantanal in Brazil is the world's largest tropical wetland and home to around 500 species of bird. It is here the hyacinth macaw (*Anodorhynchus hyacinthinus*) can be found. Easily recognisable by its distinctive electric-blue hue and yellow-ringed eyes, the hyacinth macaw is one of the largest parrot species. Sadly, though, its numbers are fast declining. With habitats destroyed by deforestation and many being captured and sold as exotic pets, the hyacinth macaw's plight is made worse by the fact that its choice of home is extremely limited.

More than 90 per cent of the birds' nests are built inside a single type of tree – the manduvi (*Sterculia apetala*) – and of that, the selection is narrower still. It is often only inside ancient manduvi trees (aged over 60 years), with sturdy hollow barks and large, shaded canopies, which these parrots choose to nest in.

Thankfully, the hyacinth macaws can rely on the diet of another tropical bird to ensure their habitat is not lost. The distinctive toco toucan (*Ramphastos toco*), with its large, flaming orange bill, is extremely fond of manduvi fruits, and is responsible for dispersing over 80 per cent of the tree's seeds. Preferring to hop from branch to branch rather than fly, the toucan's oversized beak is capable of picking hard-to-reach fruit and nuts. It digests the seeds whole, meaning they are not damaged whilst dispersed.

Unfortunately for the macaw, manduvi fruits are not all the toco toucans eat. They also prey on the hyacinth macaw's eggs, destroying over half of those laid each year. Hyacinth macaws only lay two eggs and often raise just one healthy chick, and so this is especially disastrous. In this way, the toucans are both helpful and harmful to the macaw population.

This uniquely complex relationship has been called a 'conservation puzzle' by scientists. It highlights the importance of truly understanding an ecosystem in order to protect it.

Bromeliad Tree Frogs & Bromeliads

The tropical rainforests of Central America are subject to intense heat and torrential rain showers. In fact, it rains so often here that more than 200 centimetres of rainfall are recorded each year. This damp, nutrient-rich environment means that over 500,000 species of plant and animals can be found here, accounting for the highest number of species in one concentrated area in the world.

Whilst taller trees catch much of this rainfall, some of it makes its way down through the canopy to the forest floor. Bromeliads (*Bromeliaceae*), known for their thick, waxy leaves, act as the ideal umbrellas for creatures caught in the passing showers, but these surprising plants also have a much more special role in these rainforests. Strong and curved, the leaves of the bromeliad act as tiny funnels, guiding rainwater to a basin in the plant's centre where it is stored. Scientists have discovered that over 250 different types of insects, frogs, spiders and worms have been found on these plants, which means they are a haven for wildlife. This shows just how specific symbiosis can be – where one little plant can benefit the whole animal network.

Although many types of tree frog engage in similar behaviour with puddles on the ground, one species has developed such a special relationship with bromeliads that it was named the bromeliad tree frog (*Dendropsophus bromeliaceus*). This tree frog has adapted to lay its eggs solely on bromeliad leaves, where the accumulated rainwater provides a perfect pool, packed with nutrients and safe from predators. The bromeliad provides the ideal location for the frog to lay its tiny eggs. It is thought the tadpoles live here throughout the entirety of their larval phase (before they grow legs and arms). These special bromeliad nurseries support hundreds of new tree frogs as they start their journey in life.

Leafcutter Ants & Fungus

In a line extending up to 30 metres across, an army of leafcutter ants (*Atta colombica*) marches across a damp jungle floor in South America, each carrying a piece of leaf like a warrior carries a shield. Working together, they can strip an entire tree of its leaves in just a few short hours. But these ants aren't soldiers, they are farmers.

It would seem likely that each ant is carrying a leaf for its meal, but the leaves are not for eating. First, the ants clean the leaves, then crush, cut and arrange them in an underground chamber. Here, they tend to the leaves as they begin to rot until a fungus begins to grow on the compost heap. It is this fungus that the ants feed on and on which the colony relies to survive.

As these 'fungus gardens' can develop and grow, some to well over the size of a football, it is of no surprise that the maintenance of this crop is demanding and that it requires cooperation and organisation. Leafcutter ants are highly social insects and they communicate via vibrations and sounds to ensure order and efficiency throughout the colony. Different roles are delegated to the worker ants depending on their age and size. Large ants use their powerful mandibles (jaws) to saw leaves, small worker ants seed the leaves with fungus, whilst others protect and guard the nest. It is vital that the ants work together to cultivate the garden and keep it clean and free of pests – disease could be fatal to the whole colony. The fungus is so important to the ants that the queen will take a pellet of it with her when she leaves to begin a new colony.

Because the fungus cannot survive without the ants, nor the ants without the fungus, this relationship is said to be mutualistic. This relationship is thought to date back over 50 million years, originating in the Amazon basin. These ants were perhaps the first farmers, growing and cultivating crops long before humans did.

Three-Toed & Sloths & Algae

Sometimes symbioses develops in ways that are completely unforeseen; ways that are so unique to each individual creature and habitat that it is a relationship that can never be repeated elsewhere. Take, for example, the three-toed sloth (*Bradypus variegatus*) and algae.

Found throughout Central and South American rainforests, three-toed sloths are well-known for their relaxed lifestyles. A nutrient-poor diet made up of leaves and shoots means these creatures have low energy levels and so are extremely slow moving. They are often found sleeping or resting in the jungle canopy, hanging from branches with their strong, curved claws, or draped around tree trunks. The Spanish-speaking locals often refer to them as 'los perezosos' – the lazies.

A combination of the sloth's slow movements, long hair and the damp, warm environment it inhabits has led to the development of an unusual symbiotic relationship. The sloth's hair provides the perfect conditions for algae to grow. In fact, a whole ecosystem is sustained just within its coat. This garden of algae provides a home and food for several species of small moth, and it is common that one sloth may be host to over 100 of these insects. The relationship between the sloth and the algae has become so intimate that this species of moth is found nowhere else in the world.

The moths don't start life in the sloth's fur, but in the sloth's dung. Sloths leave the confines of their leafy home once a week, climbing down to the forest floor to go to the toilet. The moths lay their eggs in the dung, and once they hatch they fly back up to the canopy to look for a sloth host. The algae on the sloth's fur provides the perfect source of nutrients that the moths need to survive. While the moths and algae thrive in this warm, wet environment, the relatively defenceless sloths benefit from a green camouflage to protect them from predators as they move slowly through the treetops.